I0108848

Words I've Never Sent

Erin Lynn
ELS Poetry

Author: Erin Lynn ELS Poetry

On Instagram @ELS_Poetry_

Photography by: Erin Lynn

Illustrations by: her daughters

💜 Bird and Bear 💜

Copyright © 2017 ELS Poetry

All rights reserved.

ISBN: 0692990690
ISBN-13: 978-0692990698

DEDICATION

This book is dedicated to everyone who went out and bought my first book, and to all of my followers on Instagram. I am so grateful for the support, reading your comments, hearing your feedback, and being able to read and enjoy a lot of your work as well. I hope you enjoy this book.
It is also dedicated to every person who came into my life and to those who left it.
The lessons I've learned from the negative people are just as valuable as the ones I've learned from the people who love me.
I owe everyone a thank you.
Thank you for loving me, thank you for hating me, for lighting this fire under my ass and giving me so much to write about.
For all the negative people thank you for showing me EXACTLY who I don't want to be, and who I don't want my children to be. I am so proud to be filled with optimism and happiness. It is effortless for me because of you.
To those who love me, you are my home, all of you, and I could never express how deeply it touches my heart and how much it means to me to be supported, loved, and understood.
My life has meaning because of you.
My most heartfelt and sincerest gratitude goes out to all of you.
Thank you.

My poems were my diary
It was there for everyone
Screaming out loud
"THIS IS WHO I AM"
It was the most vulnerable
I've ever been
And the most liberated
I've ever felt.
~Erin Lynn~

Chapter 1

The Love

JOKER

It happened like that, all those days
I thought meant something
Turned into vague memories
leaving me to wonder if they were ever even real

you *flipped*
the switch on me
But you started all of this
I think that's what kills me
I wasn't looking for you, for anyone.
You rearranged my heart and my mind.
I fell for your gazes, your words,
this invisible pull
that knocked the breath right out of me
every time you looked at me.
The way you moved toward me
like it was all you could do not to touch me
I felt it too.
You dealt those cards
And I went all in

But *you* folded.

~

<u>BEBS</u>

He wrapped his arms
Around all of my insecurities

And *kissed*

them with his.
I've never known love like this
And would never find love like it again.

~

<u>EXIT</u>

He wanted to get lost in her
In all the places he could find
In every open door, every open crease
He wanted to climb in there and stay
But he knew somewhere

in the maze of her *Heart*

there would eventually be nowhere to go but out
and he didn't think he could handle that,
The day he finally had to leave
The day things turned black
And the only lit path was neon orange from an exit sign
That was asking him gently to go
And to close the door behind him as he left.

~

<u>VACATE</u>

I struggle between
Wanting you
and wanting to be rid of you
It's a daily battle for me
Some days I wake up
and you're the first thing on my mind
before coffee
(and that's serious).
Then other days I wake up and hope
that I can get through the day
without hearing your name,
because I don't want to think of you at all.
I find myself tipping the scales of yes and no,
love and hate, and stay or go.
Maybe it's better the lack of effort you give,
it makes my decision much easier.

~

DISSIPATING

All the pieces and places
she used to think of you
are becoming increasingly

Smaller

harder to see, harder to find
and harder to touch
And I bet you didn't know
The open space in her heart
that was meant for you
is closing
Just as fast as it opened
With a lock that will never be bound
Or broken
For you again.

~

DANDELION DREAMS

I wished on all the dandelions

A little girl with a *Dream*

With all my breath watching the pieces fly
Like cotton cloud dreams up into the sky
I dreamed of you before I knew you existed
The day I met you the breeze
blew right through my heart
Like those dandelion pieces floating through
the air
You so gracefully touched my life
out of nowhere
I feel it so much and so deep
You're kissing my thoughts
while I sleep
Trapped in this place
between what's real and a dream
A never-ending burning in our hearts
we can't deny
This love is going to kill us the day we say
goodbye.
~

FALLING WITHOUT A PARACHUTE

This *falling,*
I can't tell if it's for you
Or towards the ground
Either way
It's going to hurt.

~

EMPTY HANDS

Trying to hold water in my hands,
That's what loving you felt like,
No matter how hard I tried
I was always left

With *Empty* hands.

~

MICHAELANGELO

I became your canvas
Your work of art
Everything you wanted

to put *color* into

Everything you wanted
to tear apart.

~

<u>CALLUS</u>

Your hands
The ones that shake me and steady me
Do you **understand?**
You're everything that I need
And everything I don't.

~

<u>SOAKED TO THE SKIN</u>

She was *Brave*

She dove in head first

She drowned herself in you

And you,

You were too scared to get wet.

~

<u>FLUTTERS IN MY HEART</u>

You came to me

in my dream

And when I woke up

You were gone

And so were your butterflies

Strange

How often they visit me

When you look into my eyes.

~

I TRIED

I tried to

convince myself

That the way you looked at me
Wasn't love.
I believed it
Until I saw you again.

~

<u>LIQUID COURAGE SNEAKING UP ON YOU</u>

Swallow me down
I go down nice and smooth
Like whiskey, or tequila
But more elegant,

Like a *brandy*

And you'll drink enough for two
Because I'm already drunk off you.

~

<u>IGNITE</u>

And in the darkest parts of myself

I found *You*

Sitting there waiting for me

To turn on the lights.

~

TRENCH COAT AND UMBRELLAS

I am the storm

That will bring a

Reckoning

And you my love

Don't know how to swim.

~

FALL EVERY TIME

I've seen
through you
a million times
And a million times
Still,
I fall right into you

~

TWIN FLAME

It's the rain pouring on my window
A *Melancholy*
kind of love
It's the sad song on repeat
The dream I can't remember
The clock that doesn't move
The incessant impatience in my head
And the knowing I should be through
But then its
The warmth of the sun on my face
An eccentric wild kind of love
The smile I can't hold back
The butterflies in my stomach
The look you have when you look me in my eyes
The dream I can't wake up from
And the answers I need to find
It's goodbye waiting to happen
A once was, or could've been
It's the aching in my heart that will find you
If we ever live again.

~

<u>OUR STORY</u>

And so,

Our *Story* goes

One day at a time.

~

MOVE INTO ME

Move,
Make your way to me
So, I can whisper softly in your ear

All the things you *Want* to hear

So, I can hold you tighter than ever before
Till you can't bear to leave me anymore.
~

SOULS ON FIRE

How did this happen?
Out of nowhere
This soul connection

This chemistry
Tying us together
Ripping us apart piece by piece
Day by day
And we knew it wouldn't stop
Until we had each other
Until we tasted this dream
Yes, it was love
Crazy, inexplicable, undeniable,
amazing, agonizing love
Locked up behind the cages of our ribs
Deep down inside
begging to get out
Every time we looked
Into each other's eyes
It was there
Just waiting to be kissed
Waiting to be set free
This love, this desire
Burning inside for you and me.
~

<u>CODE BLUE</u>

Subconsciously
Without realizing
You will look for pieces of me
In other people.
The pieces of me that you miss
You will look,
But you will

Never

find me.

~

<u>CAROUSEL</u>

It's a merry go round of emotions
A carnival ride that never stops,

An *endless*

ticking clock
A kaleidoscope of colors
Streaming through my mind
All the time
And it won't stop
It never stops.

~

CARAMEL

And there are times
I wish this game would just stop
And you'd come back to me

with those *Eyes*

And stare through my soul like you do
Come on, go ahead
And try to tell me you don't feel that.

~

<u>YOU ARE KILLING ME</u>

I've had moments like it
Or so I thought
That feeling that wouldn't go away
No matter how hard I fought
Where it feels like you're flying
Emotions you can't stop

There is no *Denying*

Though I'm trying
It's an endless spinning wheel
I'll never be able to explain this connection
The way you make me feel
I could never put it into words
What it is you do
Every time your hazel looks into my blue.

~

<u>MARATHON</u>

There has been whispers and sounds
Inside of me
That I could never make out
Whenever you are around
I realized today
It's my heart telling me to

Run

I just can't tell if it wants me to run toward you
Or away.

~

<u>SERENADE ME</u>

I think
if we put our hands
on each other's chests
We would slowly realize
Our bodies vibrate to the same beat

We are *Singing* the same song.

~

<u>HURRICANE</u>

You were the chaos and calm I needed
I was the storm you were waiting for
Won't you hurry back to me baby
Come on, come

dance

In our rain with me.

~

WEIRD SCIENCE

Sometimes when I think of you so randomly
It's so strong that I know
Wherever you are you must feel it
It's like I feel you thinking of me too
It's electric, beyond science,
beyond anything I could ever explain
like you've always had a piece of me
dormant inside of you
that woke up the day you met me
and from that day on

my body *Ached*

for that piece of itself back
as long as it stayed tangled up in you.

~

LOCKET

I was a *secret*

He was the key
The only one
who could open me.

~

<u>HOME</u>

I take my place of rest
In your heart,
Ever after

It's my *home* now

And I never want to leave.

~

MATCHES

It was dangerous
It was *trouble*

set on fire
And I couldn't wait
To burn with you.

~

DON'T STAND TOO CLOSE TO ME

I sometimes think loving you is a test
Meant to destroy me if I fall.
In my gut, I feel like I know this.
And still,

I can't stop

I'm fine until I see you.
When I see you
I feel gravity pulling my heart
Trying to make it collide with yours
And I collapse,
I collapse every time.

~

ISOLATION

The actions we took
To avoid one another
To run away from
what we knew we couldn't take
The love of a stranger

And the *fear*

of making a mistake.

~

TELL ME

I didn't want you to twist
Yourself into a pretzel for me
I just wanted you to want it enough
I wanted to feel you trying
If you missed me I wanted you to show it
If you were thinking about me
I wanted you to tell me
I didn't need much
I just wanted to feel you fighting
I needed to know that it mattered
I wanted you to

say it out loud

That it wasn't just me for you
That it was you,
you for me too.

~

CRYSTAL

Behind her eyes so blue

Lies a *secret*

That only you knew.

~

AUTUMNS SONG

The sun was so bright I couldn't see
The wind was making songs
With the whistling leaves
I knew it was you standing there

When I suddenly couldn't breathe

Waiting in the sun
Just looking at me
Tired and restless are we ever gonna try
Trying sounds good,
But we are better at goodbye.

~

PERSERVERE

It's scary all of it
I'm not *fearless*
about any of this
I just know that if we let this go
Right now, today
We will always regret it
I don't even know what I want,
What you want?
All I know is that I'm not ready
To give up
just yet.

~

RAIN AND RAINBOWS

You scare me
And you excite me
Like the storm I'm afraid of
Like the

Rainbow

I wait for.

~

<u>SOUND OF SILENCE</u>

I carried your name
On my tongue so

carefully

Afraid to let it out too carelessly
Afraid someone would see
How much you really meant to me.

~

<u>HOLD</u>

With closed fists
And tight grips
We *held*

onto each other
So, scared of what would be left of us
If we ever let go.

~

KISS ME

And I bet that
All the questions we have

Will be *Answered*

The second your lips touch mine
And I would also bet that
These answers are the best ones
That we are ever going to find.

~

SERENDIPITY THAT FOUND ME

I'll never forget that day in the hall

The day that started it all

You stood there in the center of the room
Your eyes caught mine
And you held them the whole time
When I looked away to walk through the door
I felt something
I could not ignore
Who was that guy
That just looked through me
This guy my body would now crave to see
I knew at that moment we were a serendipity
Unwanted, unplanned, unsought
With everything inside me coming alive
I knew you were a love I'd never survive.

~

<u>UNCONSCIOUS LOVE</u>

He woke up

This *piece*

of my heart
That all this time
I never knew was sleeping.

~

PERFECT STRANGER AT THE BAR

"I was

enchanted

to me you"
He said, as he kissed my hand
And walked out of my life.

~

SHE LOVES YOU TOO

All the ways he needed her
Came at him in the dark
His eyes wide open
Light keeps him awake from this spark

A *dream* he couldn't put out

A dream he didn't want to give up on
A girl he didn't want to be without
Her hair through his fingers
Her scent on his face
The body ache that lingers
But he's alone in this place
He closes his eyes to see her
To envision all he can
Hoping someday she'll come find him
So, they can be together again.

~

<u>HORIZON</u>

You were like her sun

You would *Rise*

And set for her
And she wilted
And bloomed for you.

~

ALPHA AND OMEGA

You left but in my chest
You remained

Beating

with my heart
Like you did

From the very start.

~

UTOPIA

And all the love
Our two souls had
Drifted away into the sky
And the hue of iridescent tones
It left behind
Like a sad song we wanted to sing
But couldn't find the words
We just walked away knowing
That without the other
Our skies would

never be

That beautiful to look at again.

~

PHOENIX

In my dream last night
You kissed me
We were standing there
In a parking lot
It was dark
And it started to rain
You said something so casual and small
I wanted to yell at you
Standing there
Looking at you, looking at me
I just had to get away from you
But you walked up to me

And you *kissed* me

In that second
We had fate
In the palm of our hands

And we felt it
And we knew that we felt it
Our souls set fire to the ground
We were standing on
We stood there burning in love
Till there was nothing left of who we were
We were reborn from the ashes
And we knew
We knew we could only burn like this for each other.

~

SAY IT

It's one of those moments
That you can't explain
That you try really hard to
But, no matter what
You can't find the words
Because there aren't any
To describe what you're feeling
In complete sincerity
It's like, in every single language
All over the world

There is no *vocabulary*

at all
To describe how deep
And how much you feel
Every single time
He says your name.

~

SHE WAS JUST A WISH

Spaghetti straps and blue jeans
A contagious laugh
And her heart on her sleeve

She was a *promise* for tomorrow

That you couldn't wait to keep
A heart you know miles away
Painful still,
You can't let her go.

~

KNIGHT

I struggled with it every day
The sense of not knowing
What to do, or where to go
Or how to push these feeing's aside
It's like your heart
Feels so much at once
And you don't know
What is right anymore
Or what to do
Because, your brain and your heart
Are going at each other like

Rivals

So, it's a daily struggle
To decide which way to move
It's like the most complicated game of chess
But you're the pawn Your heart is always the
pawn.

~

LET ME HEAR IT

It was my

favorite sound

That rolled off
the tip of your tongue
(*my name*)

~

<u>DO YOU HEAR ME</u>

I speak to you in rhymes
You're my poetry

My muse

The way I put my words
To good use.

~

I WANT YOU

Don't ever be so arrogant

As to think I need you

I never needed you

I wanted you

There is a

difference

I'm here with you

Because I want to be

Not because I have

Nowhere else to go.

~

FULL

My heart
is so full
of you
That I

forget

What I feel like.

WILD LOVE

Yes, she's emotional and wild and crazy
She's untamable
She will come into your life
And shake it up
You will love it and hate it
You will fear it and want it
God, will you want it.
And when she leaves
Because, she will leave
Make no mistake
You will

Undeniably love her

More than you ever thought possible
And you'll find it in the fragments
She leaves behind
That she was unconditionally, irrevocably
In love with you too.

~

<u>JIGSAW</u>

And the truth is
I don't even know
what I want from you
you're so confusing
Sometimes I just want you
To stay so far away from me
Then other times I want you to kiss me.
But most of the time
I just want you to tell me

Anything

that means something
Just so I know
that I'm not in this
all by myself.

~

KISMET HOLD

I knew it was something
Bigger than me
Bigger than you
This pull
This hold on us

We were *More*

than ordinary
Ordinary could never feel this way
This scary
This bad
This fucking amazing.

~

DIZZY (FULL POEM)

I knew it was wrong
And that didn't sit well with me
But no matter what I did
Or where I tried to turn
You were always there in my mind
Sitting there in my heart
It was like you came into my life
And everything changed
My whole world got flipped

Upside down

Everything I thought I knew
Everything I thought I was happy with
Suddenly just seemed like just a few pieces
Like all this time
I wasn't being my complete self
You came into my life
And I realized pieces of me were missing
That I didn't even know were mine.

~

CRASH INTO ME

It felt so far away
Maybe it felt that way
Because we were scared
But it was there for us
Close enough for us to touch
If we could just be

Brave

enough
To reach out our hands
And grab it.
~

LAUGH LIKE YOU ARE ALIVE

"I wanted to hear him laugh" she said
"harder than he'd ever laughed before

the kind of *Laugh*

that echoes and shakes
and leaves you breathless wanting more,
I want to hear him laugh like that."

~

RUNNING FAST

I was chasing you
With no intention to keep you
I *didn't* know

If that was what you wanted
Or if I was just being cruel.

~

SHE LAUGHS

"You are an array of colors" he said

"In my world that wad black and white

You painted it with your

laugh"

<u>DAYDREAM</u>

Configured in puzzles

Written in

Rhymes

You touch my cheek

I close my eyes

Your lips to mine

Touch the sky

The whole world is ours tonight.

~

<u>MAYBE</u>

Maybe there was too much inside of us

Maybe it was all in our heads

Maybe it was love

Maybe it was boredom

Maybe we would do this

And be full of regret.

I don't know

But one thing I was sure of is,

Neither of us could let go

Not really,

Not yet.

And maybe

I didn't know what that meant

But I knew that it meant something.

BEAUTIFUL DISASTER

Of all the poems I've ever written
The most beautiful ones

Were with *you*

Lying at the root of them.

~

<u>DIDN'T WE LOVE</u>

Its bittersweet isn't it?
The way I'll always be there
Stuck in the corner of your mind
And the way
You'll always be stuck in mine

Its *bittersweet*

the letting go
isn't it?
We sure loved though
Didn't we?

ENAMORED

And the truth is as

Confusing

as it gets
The second I see you
I feel different
The way you look at me
When you see me
The way I look at you
We are excited
We can't hide it
We both see that in each other
So that is what I hold onto
When I start feeling like this is nothing
Because I have faith in what I see
Your eyes looking at me
That's real
I feel it in my bones.

~

WHAT WE ARE

I don't know

What we are
At times
We are so perfect
Then we violently fall
I just can't wrap my head around it all.

<u>WE DID FALL</u>

The bottom line is we did fall.
For each other's smiles,
the gestures
The little glimpses that we got
Of each other's hearts and minds
Without a single kiss and without words.
Even now in the silence

We're still falling.

You've thought of me today,
At some point, you've thought of me.
And I've thought of you
And that's just going to have to be enough
Because no matter what road we choose
The ending is going to be the same.
It doesn't change the fact that some days
My thoughts will begin and end with you.
And it doesn't change the fact
that we don't deserve this,
This search for something we'll never be able to hold.
I hope one day we find each other again
even if it's in another lifetime.
And I hope that day is a day
we are more than dreams,
more than magic,
more than memories
I hope that day we discover this is our time
Where we can't be broken
Where we won't have to let go.

THE ONE

I wish I could tell you what it was I saw in you that day
I wish I could understand why I thought
it was so much more than it really was.
Maybe I was lacking something in my life,
And you just felt like the something I was missing.

I don't know.

But I do know that when someone is in your life
the way you've been in mine
they become a part of you.
Do not misunderstand
I'm ready for you to go.
You've had one foot out the door from the start.
And I know even if you care,
even if it's more than just a little,
you'll walk away and be fine,
and I too will be just fine.
But you will carry a part of me with you forever now,
just as I will carry apart of you with me.
You will see things and think of me.
Hear things and think of me,
things you once ignored
will stand out to you
because even though
we want to wish each other away, we can't.
Everything around us has changed now,
and so have we.
And maybe that's all we were meant to be for each other.
Maybe we will never understand why.
It's so easy to say love when it comes at you the way this did.
So infatuating, so strong and .so unexpected
But maybe, just maybe none of this was anything more than a
lesson for you and for me.
To realize how lucky we actually are,
and to stop taking for granted what we've had all along.
To stop thinking we were what we were missing.
After all we've been without one another for this long. What's
another life-time.

WE'LL NEVER KNOW WHAT COULD'VE BEEN

You used to live in my heart
Till our chances faded
one after the next
And your opportunities to tell me
while I still held on
slipped through your fingers
like water that you tried to hold

but *never* could.

I wanted us to be solid
At least in our minds
I needed to hear words worth saying
So that I had something to hold onto.
Instead it was emptiness
Over and over
that filled up the parts of my heart
where you used to live.
Now you're burned in my brain
Just a memory
Left alone lingering in its own
little compartment called
"could've been"

Seated right next to
despair and regret.
As far as I'm concerned
Inside of me
This is your home now.

~

<u>RENDER ME SPEECHLESS</u>
<u>ALMOST</u>

There are so many things
I want to say to you
Yet so many things
I cannot bring myself to say.
Isn't that always the way though?
You feel things
and you know they're real,

But *bravery*

isn't always easy.
It clashes with our insecurities
Bathes them like rain.
I want you baby, so bad.
But you scare the hell out of me.

~

<u>RESTLESS</u>

And tonight,
I won't dream about you
That's what I tell my heart
You're there
over and over again
in my mind
Even in the unconscious realm
You find a way

To waste my time.

~

WONDERLAND

Even I pondered
How so much of me
Could stay so incredibly

lost

Inside of you
And even you pondered
Why you couldn't bring yourself
To show me the way out.

~

Chapter 2

The Hurt

and the

Letting go

LATE NIGHT CRASHING

An echo in the night

Deep sea of waves crashing

Or is it the beats of my heart

Washing *Away*

every last thought of you.

~

<u>LINGER</u>

If only the memories of you

left

As easily as you did.

~

<u>ON THE ROCKS</u>

The night falls heavily on my eyelids
A handful of tequila
A heart full of

Regret

The ice clashing in my glass
Helping me forget.

~

<u>UP IN SMOKE</u>

It's true
What you don't know
will save you from some pain.
But I'm not scared of pain like that.
I've been burned by loves like yours before
I'm not scared of your matches
Your embers may burn me
But your inferno

Is no different

Than the others that I let
Smolder and burn out in my heart.
~

LOST BOY

I won't chase your shadow
This isn't Neverland
And my name is not
Peter Pan.

~

WE ARE OUT OF TIME STRANGER

You're starting to feel like a stranger
This man I couldn't wait to see
I don't want you standing outside my door
Undecided, waiting for me to come to you
If you want to be in my life
Knock, knock while you still can
Because
You're falling further and further away from me
The distance is growing, the waiting
Is taking every last piece of us
And burying it in the ground
Its making me forget

The *silence*

you barely make a sound
So, it's all slipping away
It's time for you to go now
You can't stay
I lock my doors at night
And set the alarm
It doesn't open with charm
And besides,
I don't talk to strangers.

~

<u>WEIRD</u>

This holding on
And letting go

It's *weird* isn't it?

How we can do them both
At the same time.

~

DEPARTURE

In the still of last night
During a pause

I let you go

All of it
That fast
The pain came in like a wave
And went right back out
No fleeting moment
of painful doubt
Just gone as fast as it came
I thought I'd fight more for it
Instead I sat there relieved
I didn't even cry
Sitting there
So blissfully unaware
That my heart was so ready
To say goodbye.

~

<u>THIS IS THE END</u>

I'm running on empty

Chasing a *ghost*

I'm tired of waiting

We were so close.

~

THE DANCE IS OVER

See that's the difference

between you and me

With this dance we do

You revel in the *Attention*

And the dream of it all

I wake up, turn the music on

And start to move

All the while you're still asleep

So, when you finally wake up

You realize the dream is over

But so is our song

And now, I'm gone.

~

SKYDIVING INTO ME

It was bittersweet

To say goodbye

All this time

I had my wings

I didn't know the reason why

I needed you so badly

Was because you were the one

Who would teach me how to fly.

~

AND SO IT GOES

She was an open book of dreams
Honesty, bravery, and love
With magnificent

Promise

for his tomorrow
That he didn't take the time to read
He let the pages get dusty
And the seams eventually tore
And everything that made him feel alive
Dissipated in the book
that bound his heart
It was an effortless task to read her
And even though he deeply yearned
to read these chapters
And get lost in her story
His fear
of never wanting to leave it
Kept him from getting past the first page
A beautiful plot
of two beautiful people
Left unread on a shelf
That in his heart
would forever leave an aching
Because it was supposed to be hers
for the taking.

~

<u>DUST PAN</u>

I can't believe this is the end

I'm okay, I'm fine

Don't come back anymore

My heart will

shatter

into a thousand pieces

As it hits the floor.

~

THIS IS NO INTERMISSION

You make no effort

So that's why I'm done

I didn't come here to watch you run

Your circles are making me dizzy

And frankly, I'm just too busy

To sit around waiting for the next

game to start

If you wanted me around you'd make the time

If I'm the last thing on your mind

That's all I needed to know

I'll be checking out before your next show.

~

EPIPHANY

We couldn't even be friends anymore
That's where falling in love brought us
We were stuck in an in between place
But the truth is I wanted you as a friend
more than anything

Just a *friend*

I just wanted to be a part of your life
I wanted to laugh with you
I wanted to know since you didn't drink coffee
How you took your tea
I wanted to hear about the stuff you did yesterday
What made you smile, what made you mad?
I wanted to make fun of your stupid haircut
And tell you how lame your taste of music is
While I sing it to you anyway
I wanted you to know about my day
And for you to make fun of my music
And my complete absurdity

I wanted you in such a normal way
That I realized it wasn't normal at all
I was in love with you
And you were in love with me
That is why you left
That is why we are nothing
Because we didn't know
how to be anything else anymore
And that is what kills me
Because as much as I wish I didn't
I miss you.

~

<u>PIGSTY</u>

How dare you break down my walls

Then walk away

Sledgehammer at your side

Leaving me with

nothing

But the mess you left behind.

~

<u>FEELINGS</u>

He stole my heart so effortlessly

It was as if it had been waiting for him

all this time

And, I *hated* it

I hated my heart for loving someone

That I just wanted to forget.

~

<u>ROLL THAT DICE</u>

You're playing russian roulette

with my heart

It's my fault though

I should have *never*

Put it on the table

from the start.

~

RIPTIDE

It drifted

Like something was lost at sea

Like a message in a bottle

That would never be opened

It *silenced*

the waves of my heart

Till finally all that was left

Was an undercurrent of regret

For the time spent wasted

Swimming in your seas.

~

<u>LEGACY</u>

And that's all you left behind

The memory of such a beautiful

Waste of time.

~

SAVE YOURSELF

He looks at me like I'm the only one
Who can save him from something
But when I try
I don't even know
what I'm saving him from
and when he

Runs

I realize
I'm the one who needs saving
From him
And his confused heart.

~

LOOKING GLASS

And if I see you tomorrow

I will pull from inside myself

All the *courage* to avoid

Looking into the eyes

That broke me.

~

THIS IS MY RESIGNATION

We got caught up in the dream of it all

We came this far then you made me *crawl*

That's what it comes down to.
I was zig zagging past every
orange cone to get to you
But I woke up one day
and I realized I'm through
What did we do this for?
This feeling of maybe?
I must be crazy.
It isn't real
None of it, and I'm tired
I'm tired of wasting my time.
I was out of my mind
Giving in, and giving out
More of myself than you deserve
Waiting for you and losing my nerve
Because the truth is
We are nothing more than words on a screen
A stagnant cup of coffee that ran out of steam
A dead-end street
A song with no beat
The ink at the bottom of my pen
That should have never written anything more
than "the end"

~

WILD HEART

That's what him
Holding my heart
In his hands felt like

Like a *Vise*

Gripping onto wood so tight
That it splinters and cracks from the pressure
You wait for it to loosen
But you know when it does
The splinters will fall
Like little bits of your heart
Retreating
Unable to be held
Unable to be kept
Like no wild thing can.

~

FAREWELL

Don't you see

I built my

world

around you

Just for you

to leave

~

<u>LET ME SLEEP</u>

And I'm too tired to write

Too tired of everything

That has even

the slightest resemblance of

Anything

To do

With you

~

MAZE OF LOVE

The sunlight came in
pouring through my window
A sight I usually welcomed
Today it felt like it was mocking me
All I wanted was to sit in the dark
and let myself

Feel

Every inch of this pain that was
ripping though my insides.
They say your first heartbreak
is unlike any other
I couldn't shake this
no matter how hard I tried
Deep down inside it felt like part of me died
Sitting there waiting for the day to end
and the night to begin,
Just so I could sleep away this pain I was in.
I was 15 years old
I didn't really have a clue
All the things that I thought I saw in you
We weren't capable of forever then
Hell, we weren't even capable of next week
All the pressures of being a kid
spinning around at our feet
I wouldn't have wanted you
the rest of my life anyway
It's true
all the things my teenage mind thought it knew
All the tears and frustration,
All the time, and rejection
You were a lesson to be learned

And my God was it ever!
The man you lead me to was so much better
The one I was meant to stay with all my days
It was so hard to see then that love is a maze
You get lost
and then you get found again
And eventually your forever love

Is there waiting to greet you at the end.

~

ENOUGH IS ENOUGH

I gave you everything
Every part of me

You gave me nothing

As I stood there
Looking down
At my empty hands
My heart already knew
I loved myself enough
To never return to you.

~

<u>HANDS</u>

You said

"come here you

delicate thing

Let me hold your heart in my hands"

And as soon as I did

You broke it.

~

FADED OUT

I didn't just outgrow you

I outgrew myself

I was disappearing it's true

I didn't want to be some maybe

Or an almost

I refused to be your

ghost.

~

ROUNDABOUT YOU DON'T HAVE ME

You're so convinced

You don't think I have it in me

To walk away

Every single day

I get more and more sure

One foot *further*

out the door

The game is old

I got too dizzy

Spinning around in circles with you.

~

<u>NO MORE MAYBES</u>

Maybe you want to walk away

But you never truly leave

I'm giving you your out

Here it is

If you want it

Take it and go

Just don't break back into my world again

Unless you mean it.

~

<u>SAYONARA</u>

And don't forget to take it

When you leave

The token of my appreciation

For *Reminding* me

What I can do without.

~

RESILIENCE

I *erased*

his number so reluctantly
Like a band aid you knew
you had to rip off
and throw away quickly
to avoid any pain
I thought it would hurt more
I thought it would sting
Surprisingly though,
It felt like healing
I didn't really feel a thing.

~

PONDER

I want to tell you things
I get excited about things in my life
And I want to tell you
So, I would text you

Then *Regret* it

You gave me nothing
Over and over
It was then that I knew
If you don't need me
To hear those parts of you
The parts of your life
That excite you
That make you smile or laugh
If you don't think of me
in those moments at all
Then there is nothing you have
That I could ever possibly want.

~

CRICKETS

We stood there

Waiting for the other one to speak

But all that surrounded us

Was the silence

That's when I knew it was over

It was the words left unspoken

That ultimately became

Our *demise*.

~

CIRCLE GAME

We came all this way

But I came further

I was giving you all these things

And you didn't even notice

It's like you're not even looking

So, what did you come here for?

I don't have it in me to spin around

In any more circles with you

It all started so honest

So, let's end it honest too.

~

DEPRESSION

The dark cloud appeared
I couldn't see
Staring back at all
that was thrown in front of me
distant and dazed

What's his *Name?*

I don't know this person anymore
You could see the sadness peaking
Drowning him completely
The person I used to know slipping away
Days turn into nights
Weeks turn into months
A ticking clock just waiting
All the happiness fading
He doesn't mean it I have no doubt
This light of mine
He's putting out
The apology always comes
"I'm sorry I'm so sad hon"
And I can't run
I can't see
I can't stop it
The cloud that's trying to take all of me
This darkness has a name
You'll hear it in his confession
"Please God, how do I stop this depression."

~

SLAMMED

And what a position to put me in

To put me through having

Parts of you

Wanting more

Then *hating* you

For closing the door.

~

RELEASE

And all those years
I tried and tried to make him the man
I wanted him to be
Good, faithful, nice.
He was the opposite.
He never thought I'd go
Because that's what I do

I try to *fix* people

I wanted to know that I was loveable enough
To change for.
Not for him to change completely
But for him to at least become who he
claimed he was.
That day was a day he never expected
The day that I left
I'm funny like that
I will give it all I've got
Until I'm sucked dry,
And then I'm done forever.
I had nothing left
He stood there pleading with me
Crying, for me to come back
He finally was everything I wanted
But I had no energy left for him.

It was the first time in my life I felt
This strength I never knew I had.

This guy I thought I couldn't live without for
so long
I realized I could!
I could because, I was whole all by myself.
I didn't need him to think
I was lovable enough to change for
because now, I knew that I was.
So, I stood there
looking into this person's eyes
who I thought I loved for 3 years
And I felt
Absolutely nothing.
~

<u>BREATHE</u>

The more time
I try to spend talking to you
The more I realize
I don't want any of this!
You offer me nothing but quiet

Asphyxiation

It's no wonder the times
spent without you
I feel like I can breathe again.

~

FABLE TALE

We were a fable
The lesson was learning to let go
We were meant to go to 0-60
Letting go of all our inhibitions
To fall, to crash into each other
To feel

Everything

To feel these dreams
That were always meant to fade
To damn near break
And question what the hell was happening
Was this love, or were we just crazy?
To never know
And still,
To just let go.

~

<u>SCREWED</u>

How could we lose a battle
That we never even fought?
I want to say I'm sorry
But I'll never know what for.
I never asked for much from you,
You should have seen this coming,
And I should've known better.
The first time you ran

Should've been enough for me.

I want to hate you so bad
For all the things you're never going to say
But I can't
And I know I can't afford this price
That I am going to have to pay
But I want you anyway.

~

NARCISSIST

You teased me with love
You knew I needed it

And worse I wanted it from you

You started young attacking my weaknesses
Using my insecurities to trap me in your web of lies
"it's your fault" you'd say, "you did it"
"I hurt you because you hurt me,
you deserved it, you should be sorry"
And I was every time.
The first to apologize
Never to hear one in return
I learned not to care
To push your negativity to the back of my heart
"They'll be close when they get older"
Is what everyone would say
The day came where we were grown
And with you your fakeness grew
The deep demented agony
that must be your life
Trickled down onto me once more
Infused with jealousy and blind rage
I had no chance to mend what was broken
Your children suffer from your illness
And you'd never dare admit
that they do
A narcissist to the end
And you'll be your only friend.

~

WASTED

My heart is wrapped
In disappointment and tears
From what you left behind.
Yet the sound when it beats
Is still humming your name.
My brain and heart
Will battle it out tonight
One fights for you
And the other one fights for me
Either way I lose
It's another night

Wasted

on you.

~

SUCKED DRY

The power you had over me
Started to dwindle
So you pushed harder
To get it back
The harder you pushed
The further I went away
And you couldn't

understand

Why now,
When you finally cared
I no longer did.

~

ENOUGH

I didn't want to be
some after thought
you know?
Something he did once.
I always worried about that with him
That I wouldn't be enough
That I wasn't

enough

That's when I realized
He wasn't enough for me
Cause, the one who would be
Would never make me question
My worth.

~

<u>WE SHOULD HAVE WOKEN UP</u>

All the dreams we had
Faded

And every time I slept now
You were gone
You were a memory
That shifted
To the back of my mind
Along with any chance of us
It was long gone
We were long gone.

~

SLIPPING AWAY

I sit up at night, drink my tea
And write poetry,
Then I read poetry,
And I sit here and contemplate
That with all the emotions that the human body
is capable of feeling
And mine pouring out of every open crevice in
me that there is
Why the fuck it is so hard for you
To tell me how you feel?
I used to think about you all the time
Now it's just later in the day
Or just a few times at night

Baby, I know you feel it

That you are running out of time.

~

<u>SPEAK</u>

I never intended on keeping you
I know how that sounds
Even though deep down
I knew part of me would want to

I wasn't *Naïve* enough

To believe such a thing was possible.
And through everything,
The words you never said
I think are what hits me the hardest
I knew eventually you'd become just a memory
I was ready for that, you know?!?!
I was prepared for that.
I just didn't think it would be so soon.

~

GODSPEED

The ties you

Severed

were mine
As if it ever mattered
Guess we'll never know
Don't forget the frays from them
You don't want them
sticking to your shoes
on your way home.

~

PITTER PAT

Pitter pat
The beat of my heart
Do you hear it

Falling away

from you
I'm falling away from you.

~

<u>DREAMS</u>

I never wanted to wake up

When *dreams*

of you
Were all I had left.

~

THEY'RE NOT

Your

Silence

spoke volumes
I got your message
I'll file you
With all the other

Maybes

That are worth my time.

~

DOORWAY

The way you "tried" had little significance
It barely scraped the surface of who I was
I didn't know what you wanted from me
And I was

exhausted

From trying to figure you out
The door is right there
Stop standing in it
Either
Walk through it
Or out!

~

<u>BLINDFOLDED</u>

So from now on
When I see you
I will look at you
With my eyes

Closed

Because if I open them
I'm terrified
That I will fall
right back into you
All over again.

~

PREMONITION (ITS COMING)

I was all I could do that day
To look at you
Say *Nothing*

And walk out of your life.
And it was all you could do too
To stand there
Helpless
Watching me leave.

~

MAKE IT STOP

It's me
And it's you
It's *just* me
And *just* you
And it's a moment
Then it will be gone

Say it

Say it till you are brave enough to kiss me
Because it has to stop
This aching
This not knowing what to do
This coming undone
At the thought of me and you,
It has to stop

Baby,

make it stop.

~

BABY I'M FALLING AWAY

There are depths in you
That I've never seen
That I was dying to see
I wondered if you'd ever make it a point
To let me see them
And I wondered
If I had it in me
To stick around

waiting

For you to decide whether or not
You wanted me to
I felt it slipping away
My grip was loosening
And I didn't know anymore
I didn't know if I had it in me
To hold on
To this dream
To this
Abstract version
of
You and me.

FAINT HEART

I stood there screaming
My hearts shattering truth
At the top of my lungs
For the sheer hope
That you would react
And I could hear **SOMETHING**
from you

Something, that meant *Anything*

And you didn't even look up.
~

TWENTY SOMETHING PAIN

She was sad
He tried to hold her hand
She got up
Tears in her eyes
And she started

Dancing

All alone on the floor
He said, "Erin you need to talk about it."
She said
"It hurts when I breathe, I can't even sleep,
I drifted from all that I used to be,
but I'm going to be fine I'm sure."
And she danced some more
All alone on the floor.

~

ADIEU

It's funny how much
I want to hate you
I think more so because
I'm mad at myself
Because I care,

I always care

that's the problem.
But really,
I should thank you
You've given me a lot to write about
And the realization
Of what I'm better off without.

~

THE STRANGER THAT LOVED ME (MAYBE)

I felt like I said it
Every way that I possibly could
Every nice way, every angry way,
Every single emotion that was possible to feel
I felt with you all at once
I didn't know why
I went so far, further than I've ever gone
On someone who made me feel like a fool.

I just wanted to hear you say it.

That this was real, that we were real,
That you couldn't shake me
And that you didn't want to, not yet!
But you never would,
So, I had to end it
I needed this feeling to stop
I didn't want to wonder anymore
I didn't want to walk around
With you as a question mark
Constantly kissing my thoughts
Knowing that
I would never really know you.

~

<u>SHE LOVES ME (NOT)</u>

When I finally decide
I've had enough of your shit
It will be a different kind of

Loneliness

That you feel
The kind that will show up
In the most unexpected places
The kind that will throb and ache
Wrapping itself around your heart
like a shackle
But when you finally realize
it's me that you miss
I'll be over you.

~

<u>WITHOUT</u>

Just as there is no other me
There is no other you
And we are

Without.

~

<u>I WAS GONE</u>

And to his *Surprise*
This time
When I crossed his mind
I kept on walking.

(I was gone)
~

<u>YOU</u>

You gave me
too many reasons
to let go

And not enough

To hold onto.

~

CLEAN

All the broken places
You used to live inside of me
Got filled with love from another
He whispers to the traces of you
Left behind on my skin

"You *Never* deserved her"

And I feel more of you disappear
I'm almost completely clean of you.
~

THE ANSWER IS NO

You asked me to

Marry you

On one knee
This question that should have
been everything to me,
Everything I wanted to hear
Instead fell on deaf ears
The sound of your feet
running around on me for 3 years was all I
could hear.
And all I wanted
was to break you down
The way you broke me
But I wasn't like you
I could only let someone I loved
Deep into the depths of me
And you wondered why
You were no longer invited.

~

<u>CLARITY</u>

In the end
When I really thought about it
Clear headed and seriously
I was glad it was over
Whatever it was or wasn't
All of the sudden didn't matter

And I felt *Relieved*

I wanted my life back
The life that I felt slipping away
All for nothing!
Really, for nothing at all
It wasn't who I wanted to be
I took off my rose-colored glasses
And I stumbled back onto me
Exactly where I needed to be.

~

<u>GET LOST</u>

You create these wounds
And pour salt on them
Then you wonder why
I want

Nothing

To do with you.

~

<u>MY RESOLVE</u>

Here's to you
And the year we had
Or didn't.
My resolve
Was to let you go
It was the only

choice

I had left
While we both sit around
And wait for some absolution
That we both know will never come.
So, here's to you
And the year we had
Or didn't.

~

CLAUSTROPHOBIA

Where I can't move
Is what it felt like
Being stuck in my head
With all the thoughts of you

Claustrophobic

I can't breathe
I needed to get out of my own head
I needed to un love you
And I needed you to un love me.

~

WE ARE BROKEN

We were the

Craziest idea
We ever had.
Lust found us
Love kept us
Fear stalled us
And impatience broke us.

~

FOOLS PARADISE

Your silence
was like nails on a chalkboard to me
And the way you could yield it so easily
Made me think
I really never meant anything to you.
Either that or you are the biggest coward
that I have ever met.

I don't know what's worse

Missing a fucking coward
Or missing someone
who never cared about me.
It doesn't matter how you paint this picture,
I'm still the fool.

~

<u>ASH</u>

I'm *Wallowing*

It's all I want to do
I need to sit here and feel every part
Every bitter word
Every word left unspoken
Every piece of you
I need to learn to live without
Until I can't anymore
Until I'm finally clean of you
Then I will get up
Brush off the dust
You left behind
And I will never think of you again
It's a process
But it's mine
So right now
I'm wallowing.

~

Chapter 3

The Growth

the Hope

and the

Self-Discovery

MUSIC BABY

I was a child
Sitting in the back of a red car with no seatbelt
Listening to the country music on the radio
Bruce Springsteen, Madonna,
and Billy Joel.
I didn't know then that

This was just the beginning

Of music saving my life.
~

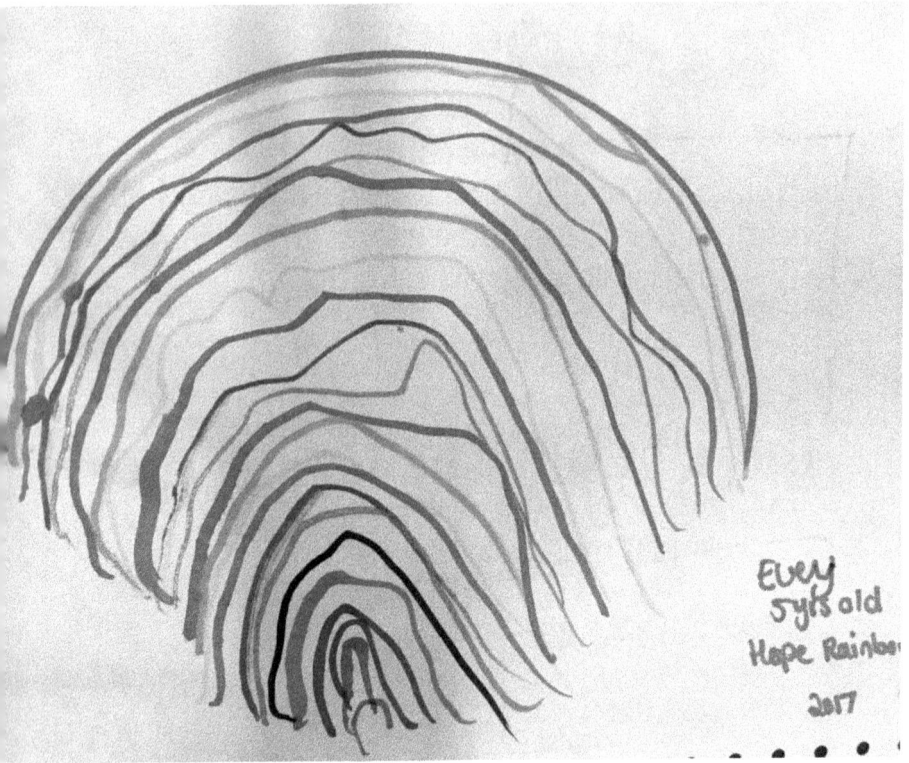

Evey
5yrs old
Hope Rainbow
2017

HOPE

You must keep going
Even though the road seems long
And your fears seem endless
Look for the light in the dark
And if you cannot find the light

Be the light.

~

FINE WINE

And I gave up
spending time with people
Who made me feel

Alone

I can drink enough for three
Me, myself and I'll be fine
As I pat my own back
And pour myself some wine.

~

TEENSTRANGER 1997

I just don't know when
to give less of

myself

I give it all I have
Too often to find
That I'm the one
Who gets left behind.

~

HIDE AND SEEK

It's not really
That I was ever
lost

I just needed more time
To find myself.

~

DEFEAT THIS

The way I learned to love myself
The replace your abuse
Shocked even me
Its why I don't hate you
While stepping over all the shattered
Pieces of my self esteem
That you threw to the ground
I stumbled onto so much

self-love

That my pieces glued themselves back together
And even cracked they were
Stronger than you could ever be
And they laughed at you
For thinking you defeated me
Only I have the power to do that.

~

<u>SELF LOVE</u>

You found me broken on the floor
You picked up my fragile heart
And you sewed it back together again
You made it your work of art
The love you poured over me
Your words so kind
Setting me free
From all the sadness and fear
You made it all disappear
I felt myself starting to

heal

All the ways you made me feel
I wanted to thank you
As I reached out to hug you
I bumped into a mirror
Surprised and taken back
Though it couldn't be clearer
"Is this true"
How could it be I never knew
This healing
This gentle hand I couldn't see
All this time
Was coming from me.

~

I BUILT MYSELF A CASTLE

All those times they thought they won
Because they made me cry
They didn't know deep down inside
My skin was getting thicker
My heart was healing quicker
And I bet they never knew
With every stone they threw
That I was building a

pedestal

One that stood harder and tougher
Than concrete
All because of the stones
They kept throwing at my feet.

~

AND SHE WAS

She cried
It was a moment
where she completely broke down, and cried.
The kind of cry that comes easily
Because you've held it in for so long.
She held her head in her hands
Until there were no tears left.
Then she brushed her hair out of her eyes
Wiped her own face

And told herself

That she was going
to be fine.

~

<u>REGRET</u>

If I regret anything in this life
It's the time that I've spent
Explaining myself to people

Who have *never*

deserved anything from me
Let alone, an explanation.

~

<u>SHEEP</u>

She dared to be different
While they all stayed the same

And they couldn't *understand*

Why she didn't remember
Any of their names.

~

NOBODYS PORCELAIN

What's impressive about her
And quite addicting is
She falls
But,
She

Never

breaks.

~

HOME ECONOMICS

There are moments when
I don't know who I am anymore
I feel *lost* in translation

Like I'm never meant to find my way
It's a struggle,
A battle
One I fight alone
and always will
I pick up my pieces
And sew them back together again
Then tomorrow,
I'll do it all over again.

~

SHATTERED

There is something to be said
About the glass half full kind of people
We are full of hope
We need that

That *optimism*

helps us get through
Our day to day
So, these glass half empty people
Come around and we want to help them
But sometimes, in that process
the pressure and negativity are too much
and they break our glass
then we must set out to fix ourselves
to mend our glass
so we can help the next person that needs us
but sometimes
through that process
we can't find all of our broken pieces
and then our glass can't hold all of the water
anymore
but we try like hell to hold onto it
to patch it up
to not stay broken
because without hope
we are all just broken glass.

IMPULSIVE

I'm definitely *not* a

"wait and see" type of girl
I know what I want in the moment
I think that means something
To move
"Now" is risky
"Never" is boring
And "maybe"
Is just a waste
of my fucking time.

~

ANYTHING BUT

That's my problem
When I care
I don't see people for who they are
I see them for who
they have the

potential to be

I give and give and give
Until I have nothing left
Till,
I'm left sitting there empty
And I wonder how,
Those who were soft hearted like me
Turned out to be anything but.

~

VOID

It's an

emptiness

you try to fill
But you can't
Because the truth is
The emptiness is an illusion
It was never really there
To be emptied or filled
We sit here waiting
For that "one"
To fill us
We say that with words
Completion, destiny
But all we are really doing is finding
someone
To help us get through the day
Someone to laugh with
Who understands the little fragments
That make us who we are
So that life's disappointments are easier to
handle
But no matter who we think "the one" is
The only person that is truly capable
Of filling that emptiness inside
Is ourselves.

2011 AND THEY SAID, "LET IT GO"

I can't stand when they tell me to

"let it go"

Like I haven't tried.
Like every day I don't wake up
And wish this feeling gone.
As if I can give anymore of myself
To this process of moving forward
I'm hanging by a thread and
You say, "let it go"
As if my feelings aren't valid
As if a person could enjoy feeling this way. `
I wish I could let it go
I wish it were so easy to piece back together
The parts of me they shattered
And stepped on with their dirty shoes
On their way out the door.
But thank you,
I'll make sure I work on letting it go.

~

<u>BURN</u>

I burn bridges often
Not because I'm bitter
Or because I feel better than anyone
But as a form of

self-protection

I'll burn it as I'm walking off it
I'll burn that bridge twice
And as the ashes fall from the sky
And the smoke envelopes my feet
I know
That once I've made that choice
I'll never regret lighting that match.

~

<u>RISE UP</u>

So young and broken back then
That was my mistake
When I fell to his feet
All of those times
In fear that without him
I couldn't be complete

And with dirty knees

One day I Rose

I was my own again
And he was no ones
And nothing to me.

~

<u>NO FILTERS</u>

I get flooded
When I'm emotional
And my words get

Scattered

They get messy and sloppy
And always, I feel too much
More than you deserve.
You're a thought that would be better left
Where I found you in the first place
I'm not sure why I say everything I feel
I guess it's because deep down I know
That if you're meant to go
In the end
What I said or didn't say
Would have never made
Much difference anyway.

~

LIGHT THE WAY

Although it may feel like it
This pain isn't permanent
Nothing in life is
It's a bittersweet reality
If you look at that in a positive way
And live your life knowing that you didn't
Fall into some black hole with no escape
There is light at the end of every tunnel

But you need to have eyes *willing*

to see the light
That can wait,
Eyes that never give up hope
That eventually that light is going to be there
AND IT'S GOING TO LEAD YOU HOME.

~

ANOREXIC LOVE

I've starved myself

From love like this before
You're not the first one
To think I'd wait forever
But you will be the last
Whatever it is you're cooking,
I'm no longer hungry.

<u>WILD</u>

I questioned it
When he left
Was I enough?
Was I adequate enough to keep?
But I was more than enough
So much enough
That he couldn't hold onto me
And in my sadness
I sunk my teeth into myself
And I tasted the wild
That he could not carry
That he could never hold
Because,
This kind of enough
Couldn't be held by just anyone
You needed to be able to
Breathe
And
Speak
Wild!

I AM MINE FIRST

I couldn't love you
I tried
You dissected my every move
I became

Unrecognizable

A vanishing act
With you in the front seat
Swallowed up into
who you wanted me to be
Your power trip exhausted me
I had nothing left inside to give
I needed to let you go
So that I could live.

~

<u>CONSTANT</u>

You

deserve

to be more
than
temporary.

~

<u>PIECES</u>

I never do anything halfway
I'm either all in
Or all out
There is no in between for me
I don't know how
To love people in
halves.

~

DANCE WITH ME

It's just always been how I do things
I go against the grain
I march to the beat of my own drum
I've never wanted to be like everyone else
Not because I think I'm better
But because,
That's how I feel like I'd lose me
A lot of people don't get me because of that
But I don't care
You see,
I can't hear what they say

Over the music my drums play.

~

<u>WARRIOR</u>

Life will indeed knock you down
But it's your job
To pull all the

Strength

From within yourself
Dust yourself off
And rise
Over and over again
As many times as it takes
For life to get the message
That you won't give in
It's not in your bones
You are powerful.

~

PAPER DOLL

She was a paper doll
You tried to hold her tight
And she crumbled

You were Sorry

You never meant to hurt her
So, you tried to fix her creases
But she started to rip
It was then you realized
You loved someone so much
That you could never hold
That could never be yours.

~

WILD FLOWER

She was born
Wild

It was something that
No one could give to her
Or take away from her.
It's how she was created.

~

LOVE YOURSELF ENOUGH

I used to be that jealous petty girl
I remember those days
You hate girls who are pretty or talented
Before you even know them

Because, you're *Scared*

"what if he likes her more than me"
We are all insecure,
Even that model in a size 0
with big boobs and round booty
She's insecure too, you know why?
Because at some point in time someone
made her feel bad about herself
made her feel inadequate, like she wasn't
enough.
No matter who you are, how pretty you are,
how talented you are
None of us are perfect.
Now that I'm a woman
and I've learned to love myself
For everything I am and everything I'm not
I am inspired by strong, powerful women.
I'm trying to raise two of them.
You can't stop any guy from cheating
By hating every girl who has something you
don't.
And hate doesn't solve any problems anywhere.
So, I will encourage my girls to embrace

everyone,
And to know, you can't control
what other people do.
Just know if they hurt you, you need to walk
away
And know, something better is waiting for you
on the other end of that pain.
But love, love so so hard
Every day no matter what
Don't let pain, or betrayal take away that light
That shines so bright inside of you.
Shine! Light up every single room that you walk
into
and never ever stop.

~

<u>YOU HAVE NO POWER OVER ME</u>

And may the disturbing

Hate and jealousy

That others throw at you
Set a fire under your ass
That makes you push harder
To make yourself even better,
Brighter, and even more amazing
than you were the first time
they tried to destroy your spirit.
Be the unbreakable phenomenal
Bad ass that you are,
And do it all
With a smile.

~

EXPOSED

She was just a

Heart

It was just her

Sleeve.

~

THE GRASS IS FINE RIGHT HERE

Whoever you are
Wherever you are
You always want
What you don't have

And the *Realization*

of that
The understanding that most times
That's all its about
The chase
Will save you from so much heartache
You never really wanted it anyway
So, breathe, realize you're fantastic
And fine, and worth so much more
Than minuscule amounts of time
Know it,
And move the fuck on.

~

THE DARKNESS HAS A NAME

I used to live
In a place that was too ugly
for anyone, a place where
sadness combed my hair
at night, and darkness
filled where there once
was light.
I used to live there
In that place
Until I realized,
only I could turn on the lights.

AT A LOSS

I had *Nothing* to say
And I'm a writer
To get me to the point
Where I have no words
Well,
You either matter too much
Or not at all.

~

<u>LUCKY YOU</u>

I won't wait
For anymore
Words from you.
I don't want to live like that

Waiting,

It's not my style.

~

<u>I CAN'T MAKE YOU LOVE YOURSELF</u>

If I were to make a list
Of all the people who had something negative
to say about me, it would be long.
As long as their list of

Insecurities

That brought my name to their mouth
In the first place
And the list of fucks that I gave
Would be short.

~

<u>FILTERS ARE FOR INSTAGRAM</u>

I will not
water down my words
and pretend to be
someone I'm not
just to please you!

If I am too *strong*

For your taste,
Get a chaser
OR FIND ANOTHER DRINK.

~

BROKEN CAGE

I will not be subdued
Chastened, hushed and solemn
I'm too alive for that

I'm too emotionally alive

For any of that.
I am cheerful, boisterous,
And wild
I'm not meant for quiet, still things
The only cage I have
is the one protecting my heart
And even that opened up for you.

~

ITS BEEN REAL

I had a million things to say
But no words
that would come anymore.

My *catastrophe*

Was being honest
I was okay with that.
And I'm not sorry
THAT YOU WEREN'T.
~

MY MUSIC MY WORDS

My music and my words
Inviting whoever is willing to

Listen

Inside, to the most intimate parts
Of my soul.

~

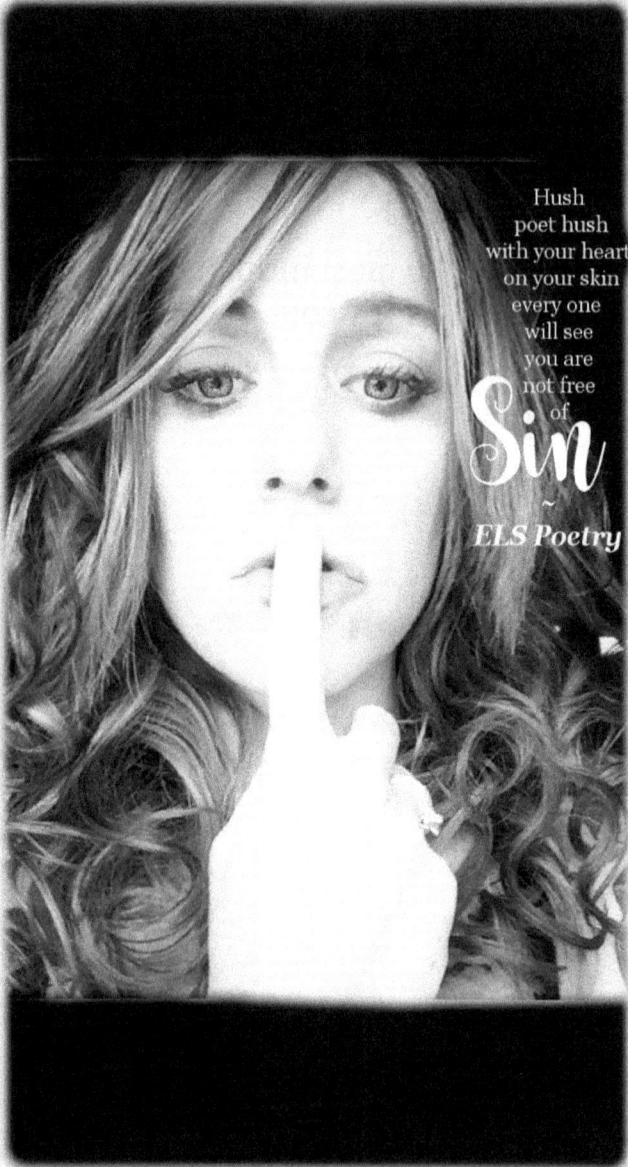

Hush
poet hush
with your heart
on your skin
every one
will see
you are
not free
of

Sin

~

ELS Poetry

ABOUT THE AUTHOR

I have always had a soft spot for the arts, specifically music, literature, anything that moved me or made me feel. I am a mother, a wife, a photographer, and a writer. I started writing poetry when I was 10 years old. For me it was a way of expressing myself in a manner I was not yet brave enough to do out loud. Through the years I sporadically continued to write when thoughts or feelings came over me. I've had lots of inspiration through my friends and family members experiences as well, which helped trigger my thoughts for creative writing. For me writing is therapy, you release how you feel, its healing in itself. I enjoy writing, as much as I enjoy reading poetry, maybe not as much as listening to music, but I do both together often, that's more my style. 😊
Enjoy, and thank you.
~Erin~

www.ingramcontent.com/pod-product-compliance
Lightning Source LLC
Chambersburg PA
CBHW061819040426
42447CB00012B/2729